The Art of

Cursive

Handwriting

A Self-Teaching Workbook

You <u>can</u> learn it.

Jenny Pearson

The Art of Cursive Handwriting: A Self-Teaching Workbook

Jenny Pearson

Kivett Publishing

ISBN: 978-1-545-17267-4

Language Arts > Handwriting

TABLE OF CONTENTS

INTRODUCTION

The main idea behind cursive handwriting is to let you write an entire word in a single smooth motion. You can see this with the example below. The word is "connected." Note how all of the letters connect to one another. You don't lift your pencil off the paper to write a new letter of the same word. You just continue from one letter to the next.

Connected

There are many benefits to learning how to write in cursive:

- It offers additional practice (beyond printing and drawing) with motor skills and general penmanship.
- You can take notes faster in cursive than in print writing.
- The knowledge will help you learn how to sign your name.
- If you come across a note or letter written in cursive handwriting, you will be able to read what it says.
- Traditionally, personal checks are written in cursive.
- You can experience the artistic element involved in forming the cursive letters.
- It can be fun to learn something new.

1

The Cursive Alphabet

Directions:

1. Study how each letter is drawn. We show you step by step our recommendation for how to write each letter.

2. First practice by tracing over the dotted letters.

3. Next write the letter several times on the blank lines below the dotted letters.

4. Try to remember how each letter looks and how to write each letter of the alphabet. When you finish this chapter, spend some time studying the letters of the cursive alphabet. It will help you later if you can remember them.

Uppercase Print A = Uppercase Cursive *a*

Write uppercase cursive *a* as shown below.

Trace the dotted letters below. Write the letter without lifting your pencil off of the page.

Practice writing the uppercase cursive *a* several times on the blank lines below. One letter is drawn as an example.

Lowercase Print a = Lowercase Cursive *a*

Write lowercase cursive *a* as shown below.

Trace the dotted letters below. Note that lowercase *a* is half the height of uppercase *A*.

Practice writing the lowercase cursive *a* several times on the blank lines below. One letter is drawn as an example.

Repetition Note

Does this chapter provide more practice than you need?

- When you feel like you have mastered a letter, feel free to advance onto the next page.

- If you're working independently, you don't need to fill out the entire page unless you feel that you need the extra practice. However, keep in mind that more practice will help you write better.

- If a parent or teacher asks you to complete the page, then you don't have a choice. You better complete the page. ☺

- Some students need more practice than other students, so there is plenty of room for those who need it.

- If you save some space now, you will be able to return to this section in the future if you later decide that you would like more practice with individual letters.

Style Note

Are your letters coming out a little differently?

- It may be okay if your letters look a little different.

- What matters most is if your letter is recognizable.

- Not everybody writes all 26 uppercase and lowercase cursive letters exactly the same way.

- In fact, different forms of the cursive alphabet are taught at different schools in different regions (and even in different time periods). There isn't a single definitive, universal way to write the cursive alphabet.

- Focus on trying to make your letters recognizable with a smooth motion. If it's a little bit off, as in the example below, it's okay.

a a

Uppercase Print B = Uppercase Cursive $\mathcal{B}$

Write uppercase cursive $\mathcal{B}$ as shown below.

Trace the dotted letters below. Note how picture 3 above begins by retracing part of the route from picture 2.

Practice writing the uppercase cursive $\mathcal{B}$ several times on the blank lines below. One letter is drawn as an example.

Lowercase Print b = Lowercase Cursive *b*

Write lowercase cursive *b* as shown below.

Trace the dotted letters below. Write the letter without lifting your pencil off of the page.

Practice writing the lowercase cursive *b* several times on the blank lines below. One letter is drawn as an example.

Uppercase Print C = Uppercase Cursive $\mathcal{C}$

Write uppercase cursive $\mathcal{C}$ as shown below.

Trace the dotted letters below. Write the letter in one smooth motion without lifting your pencil off of the page.

Practice writing the uppercase cursive $\mathcal{C}$ several times on the blank lines below. One letter is drawn as an example.

Lowercase Print c = Lowercase Cursive c

Write lowercase cursive c as shown below.

Trace the dotted letters below. Note that lowercase c is half the height of uppercase C.

Practice writing the lowercase cursive c several times on the blank lines below. One letter is drawn as an example.

c

c

c

c

Uppercase Print D = Uppercase Cursive $\mathcal{D}$

Write uppercase cursive $\mathcal{D}$ as shown below.

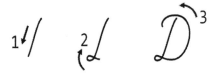

Trace the dotted letters below. Write the letter without lifting your pencil off of the page.

Practice writing the uppercase cursive $\mathcal{D}$ several times on the blank lines below. One letter is drawn as an example.

Lowercase Print d = Lowercase Cursive *d*

Write lowercase cursive *d* as shown below.

₁ C ²↑ *d* *d* 3 *d* 4

Trace the dotted letters below. First form the loop and complete the letter with an up and then down motion.

d d d d d d d d d d d d d d d

Practice writing the lowercase cursive *d* several times on the blank lines below. One letter is drawn as an example.

d

d

d

d

Uppercase Print E = Uppercase Cursive $\mathcal{E}$

Write uppercase cursive $\mathcal{E}$ as shown below.

Trace the dotted letters below. Write the letter without lifting your pencil off of the page.

Practice writing the uppercase cursive $\mathcal{E}$ several times on the blank lines below. One letter is drawn as an example.

Lowercase Print e = Lowercase Cursive *e*

Write lowercase cursive *e* as shown below.

Trace the dotted letters below. Write the letter without lifting your pencil off of the page.

Practice writing the lowercase cursive *e* several times on the blank lines below. One letter is drawn as an example.

_____

_____ℓ_____

_____

_____ℓ_____

_____

_____ℓ_____

_____

_____ℓ_____

Uppercase Print F = Uppercase Cursive $\mathcal{F}$

Write uppercase cursive $\mathcal{F}$ as shown below.

Trace the dotted letters below. First draw the top line, then the downward stroke, and finally the middle line.

Practice writing the uppercase cursive $\mathcal{F}$ several times on the blank lines below. One letter is drawn as an example.

Lowercase Print f = Lowercase Cursive _f_

Write lowercase cursive _f_ as shown below.

Trace the dotted letters below. Write the letter without lifting your pencil off of the page.

Practice writing the lowercase cursive _f_ several times on the blank lines below. One letter is drawn as an example.

Uppercase Print G = Uppercase Cursive *G*

Write uppercase cursive *G* as shown below.

Trace the dotted letters below. Write the letter without lifting your pencil off of the page.

Practice writing the uppercase cursive *G* several times on the blank lines below. One letter is drawn as an example.

Lowercase Print g = Lowercase Cursive *g*

Write lowercase cursive *g* as shown below.

Trace the dotted letters below. Write the letter without lifting your pencil off of the page.

Practice writing the lowercase cursive *g* several times on the blank lines below. One letter is drawn as an example.

Uppercase Print H = Uppercase Cursive $\mathcal{H}$

Write uppercase cursive $\mathcal{H}$ as shown below.

Trace the dotted letters below. First go down, then across to the right, and then down again. See page 81 for an alternative.

Practice writing the uppercase cursive $\mathcal{H}$ several times on the blank lines below. One letter is drawn as an example.

Lowercase Print h = Lowercase Cursive h

Write lowercase cursive h as shown below.

Trace the dotted letters below. Write the letter without lifting your pencil off of the page.

Practice writing the lowercase cursive h several times on the blank lines below. One letter is drawn as an example.

Uppercase Print I = Uppercase Cursive *I*

Write uppercase cursive *I* as shown below.

Trace the dotted letters below. Write the letter without lifting your pencil off of the page.

Practice writing the uppercase cursive *I* several times on the blank lines below. One letter is drawn as an example.

Lowercase Print i = Lowercase Cursive *i*

Write lowercase cursive *i* as shown below.

Trace the dotted letters below. First form the base of letter and then add the dot.

Practice writing the lowercase cursive *i* several times on the blank lines below. One letter is drawn as an example.

Uppercase Print J = Uppercase Cursive $\mathcal{J}$

Write uppercase cursive $\mathcal{J}$ as shown below.

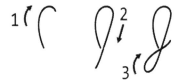

Trace the dotted letters below. Write the letter without lifting your pencil off of the page.

Practice writing the uppercase cursive $\mathcal{J}$ several times on the blank lines below. One letter is drawn as an example.

Lowercase Print j = Lowercase Cursive *j*

Write lowercase cursive *j* as shown below.

Trace the dotted letters below. First form the base of letter and then add the dot.

Practice writing the lowercase cursive *j* several times on the blank lines below. One letter is drawn as an example.

Uppercase Print K = Uppercase Cursive $\mathcal{K}$

Write uppercase cursive $\mathcal{K}$ as shown below.

Trace the dotted letters below. First draw the downward stroke, and then add the diagonal strokes.

Practice writing the uppercase cursive $\mathcal{K}$ several times on the blank lines below. One letter is drawn as an example.

Lowercase Print k = Lowercase Cursive *k*

Write lowercase cursive *k* as shown below.

Trace the dotted letters below. Write the letter without lifting your pencil off of the page.

Practice writing the lowercase cursive *k* several times on the blank lines below. One letter is drawn as an example.

Uppercase Print L = Uppercase Cursive $\mathcal{L}$

Write uppercase cursive $\mathcal{L}$ as shown below.

Trace the dotted letters below. Write the letter without lifting your pencil off of the page.

Practice writing the uppercase cursive $\mathcal{L}$ several times on the blank lines below. One letter is drawn as an example.

Lowercase Print l = Lowercase Cursive _l_

Write lowercase cursive _l_ as shown below.

Trace the dotted letters below. Write the letter without lifting your pencil off of the page.

Practice writing the lowercase cursive _l_ several times on the blank lines below. One letter is drawn as an example.

Uppercase Print M = Uppercase Cursive $\mathcal{M}$

Write uppercase cursive $\mathcal{M}$ as shown below.

Trace the dotted letters below. Note how pictures 2 and 4 begin by retracing part of the route from pictures 1 and 3.

Practice writing the uppercase cursive $\mathcal{M}$ several times on the blank lines below. One letter is drawn as an example.

Lowercase Print m = Lowercase Cursive *m*

Write lowercase cursive *m* as shown below.

Trace the dotted letters below. Write the letter without lifting your pencil off of the page. Note that there are 3 humps.

Practice writing the lowercase cursive *m* several times on the blank lines below. One letter is drawn as an example.

Uppercase Print N = Uppercase Cursive 𝑁

Write uppercase cursive 𝑁 as shown below.

Trace the dotted letters below. Note how picture 2 begins by retracing part of the route from picture 1.

Practice writing the uppercase cursive 𝑁 several times on the blank lines below. One letter is drawn as an example.

Lowercase Print n = Lowercase Cursive *n*

Write lowercase cursive *n* as shown below.

Trace the dotted letters below. Write the letter without lifting your pencil off of the page. Note that there are 2 humps.

Practice writing the lowercase cursive *n* several times on the blank lines below. One letter is drawn as an example.

Uppercase Print O = Uppercase Cursive $\mathcal{O}$

Write uppercase cursive $\mathcal{O}$ as shown below.

Trace the dotted letters below. Write the letter without lifting your pencil off of the page.

Practice writing the uppercase cursive $\mathcal{O}$ several times on the blank lines below. One letter is drawn as an example.

Lowercase Print o = Lowercase Cursive *o*

Write lowercase cursive *o* as shown below.

$$\{_1(\qquad U_j^2 \qquad O_j^3$$

Trace the dotted letters below. Note that lowercase *o* is half the height of uppercase *O*.

Practice writing the lowercase cursive *o* several times on the blank lines below. One letter is drawn as an example.

_____
O
_____

_____
O
_____

_____
O
_____

_____
O
_____

Uppercase Print P = Uppercase Cursive $\mathcal{P}$

Write uppercase cursive $\mathcal{P}$ as shown below.

Trace the dotted letters below. Write the letter without lifting your pencil off of the page.

Practice writing the uppercase cursive $\mathcal{P}$ several times on the blank lines below. One letter is drawn as an example.

Lowercase Print p = Lowercase Cursive *p*

Write lowercase cursive *p* as shown below.

Trace the dotted letters below. Write the letter without lifting your pencil off of the page.

Practice writing the lowercase cursive *p* several times on the blank lines below. One letter is drawn as an example.

Uppercase Print Q = Uppercase Cursive $\mathcal{Q}$

Write uppercase cursive $\mathcal{Q}$ as shown below.

Trace the dotted letters below. Write the letter without lifting your pencil off of the page.

Practice writing the uppercase cursive $\mathcal{Q}$ several times on the blank lines below. One letter is drawn as an example.

Lowercase Print q = Lowercase Cursive *q*

Write lowercase cursive *q* as shown below.

Trace the dotted letters below. Write the letter without lifting your pencil off of the page.

Practice writing the lowercase cursive *q* several times on the blank lines below. One letter is drawn as an example.

Uppercase Print R = Uppercase Cursive $\mathcal{R}$

Write uppercase cursive $\mathcal{R}$ as shown below.

Trace the dotted letters below. Write the letter without lifting your pencil off of the page.

Practice writing the uppercase cursive $\mathcal{R}$ several times on the blank lines below. One letter is drawn as an example.

Lowercase Print r = Lowercase Cursive *n*

Write lowercase cursive *n* as shown below.

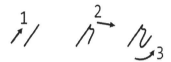

Trace the dotted letters below. Write the letter without lifting your pencil off of the page.

Practice writing the lowercase cursive *n* several times on the blank lines below. One letter is drawn as an example.

Uppercase Print S = Uppercase Cursive

Write uppercase cursive  as shown below.

Trace the dotted letters below. Write the letter without lifting your pencil off of the page.

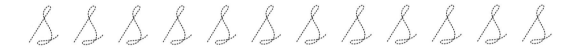

Practice writing the uppercase cursive  several times on the blank lines below. One letter is drawn as an example.

Lowercase Print s = Lowercase Cursive *s*

Write lowercase cursive *s* as shown below.

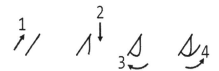

Trace the dotted letters below. Write the letter without lifting your pencil off of the page.

Practice writing the lowercase cursive *s* several times on the blank lines below. One letter is drawn as an example.

Uppercase Print T = Uppercase Cursive $\mathcal{T}$

Write uppercase cursive $\mathcal{T}$ as shown below.

Trace the dotted letters below. First draw the horizontal line and then make the downward stroke.

Practice writing the uppercase cursive $\mathcal{T}$ several times on the blank lines below. One letter is drawn as an example.

Lowercase Print t = Lowercase Cursive *t*

Write lowercase cursive *t* as shown below.

Trace the dotted letters below. First make the up and down motion and then cross it with a horizontal line.

Practice writing the lowercase cursive *t* several times on the blank lines below. One letter is drawn as an example.

t

t

t

t

Uppercase Print U = Uppercase Cursive $\mathcal{U}$

Write uppercase cursive $\mathcal{U}$ as shown below.

Trace the dotted letters below. Write the letter without lifting your pencil off of the page.

Practice writing the uppercase cursive $\mathcal{U}$ several times on the blank lines below. One letter is drawn as an example.

Lowercase Print u = Lowercase Cursive *u*

Write lowercase cursive *u* as shown below.

Trace the dotted letters below. Write the letter without lifting your pencil off of the page.

Practice writing the lowercase cursive *u* several times on the blank lines below. One letter is drawn as an example.

Uppercase Print V = Uppercase Cursive $\mathcal{V}$

Write uppercase cursive $\mathcal{V}$ as shown below.

Trace the dotted letters below. Write the letter without lifting your pencil off of the page.

Practice writing the uppercase cursive $\mathcal{V}$ several times on the blank lines below. One letter is drawn as an example.

Lowercase Print v = Lowercase Cursive u

Write lowercase cursive u as shown below.

Trace the dotted letters below. Write the letter without lifting your pencil off of the page.

Practice writing the lowercase cursive u several times on the blank lines below. One letter is drawn as an example.

Uppercase Print W = Uppercase Cursive $\mathcal{W}$

Write uppercase cursive $\mathcal{W}$ as shown below.

Trace the dotted letters below. Write the letter without lifting your pencil off of the page.

Practice writing the uppercase cursive $\mathcal{W}$ several times on the blank lines below. One letter is drawn as an example.

Lowercase Print w = Lowercase Cursive *w*

Write lowercase cursive *w* as shown below.

Trace the dotted letters below. Write the letter without lifting your pencil off of the page.

Practice writing the lowercase cursive *w* several times on the blank lines below. One letter is drawn as an example.

Uppercase Print X = Uppercase Cursive $\mathcal{X}$

Write uppercase cursive $\mathcal{X}$ as shown below.

Trace the dotted letters below. First make a stroke down to the right and then make a stroke down to the left.

Practice writing the uppercase cursive $\mathcal{X}$ several times on the blank lines below. One letter is drawn as an example.

Lowercase Print x = Lowercase Cursive *x*

Write lowercase cursive *x* as shown below.

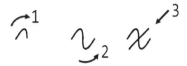

Trace the dotted letters below. Note that lowercase *x* is half the height of uppercase *X*.

Practice writing the lowercase cursive *x* several times on the blank lines below. One letter is drawn as an example.

Uppercase Print Y = Uppercase Cursive $\mathcal{Y}$

Write uppercase cursive $\mathcal{Y}$ as shown below.

Trace the dotted letters below. Write the letter without lifting your pencil off of the page.

Practice writing the uppercase cursive $\mathcal{Y}$ several times on the blank lines below. One letter is drawn as an example.

Lowercase Print y = Lowercase Cursive *y*

Write lowercase cursive *y* as shown below.

Trace the dotted letters below. Write the letter without lifting your pencil off of the page.

Practice writing the lowercase cursive *y* several times on the blank lines below. One letter is drawn as an example.

Uppercase Print Z = Uppercase Cursive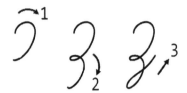

Write uppercase cursive ℨ as shown below.

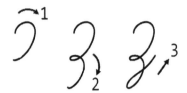

Trace the dotted letters below. Write the letter without lifting your pencil off of the page.

Practice writing the uppercase cursive ℨ several times on the blank lines below. One letter is drawn as an example.

Lowercase Print z = Lowercase Cursive *z*

Write lowercase cursive *z* as shown below.

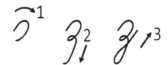

Trace the dotted letters below. Note that lowercase *z* is a shorter version of uppercase *Z*.

Practice writing the lowercase cursive *z* several times on the blank lines below. One letter is drawn as an example.

Let's review the alphabet one time. First trace over the dotted letters, and then copy the letters onto the blank line below. If your forget how to write a letter, flip back to the page that shows you how to write it.

A a B b C c D d E e F f G g

_____

_____

H h I i J j K k L l M m

_____

_____

N n O o P p Q q R r S s T t

_____

_____

U u V v W w X x Y y Z z

_____

_____

2

Tricky Letters

Directions:

1. Study the issues described in this chapter.

2. Practice tracing over the dotted letters and writing the letters on the blank lines below. If you forget how to write a letter, review the diagram from Chapter 1.

3. Try to remember the issues described in this chapter. These letters aren't tricky when you are aware of the issues and when you remember what seemed tricky about them. The sooner you master this chapter, the easier it will be to both write and read cursive handwriting.

The trickiest cursive letters are the letters that look different in cursive compared to how they look in print.

For example, compare the uppercase cursive *G* to the uppercase print G.

G G

When the cursive and print versions of the same letter appear different, it takes some practice and studying to identify the letter and to remember how to write it. This chapter provides extra practice writing cursive letters that look different from the print letters. (This chapter will also explore other ways that cursive letters can be tricky, aside from appearance.)

Some cursive letters are easier than others. For example, lowercase cursive *h* looks similar to lowercase print h. This makes it easier to identify and to remember.

h h

Compare lowercase cursive *b* with lowercase print b.

b b

Trace the dotted letters below.

b b b b b b b b b b b b b

Practice writing the lowercase cursive *b* several times.

b

Compare lowercase cursive *e* with lowercase print e.

e e

Trace the dotted letters below.

e e e e e e e e e e e e e e e e

Practice writing the lowercase cursive *e* several times.

e

Compare lowercase cursive *f* with lowercase print f.

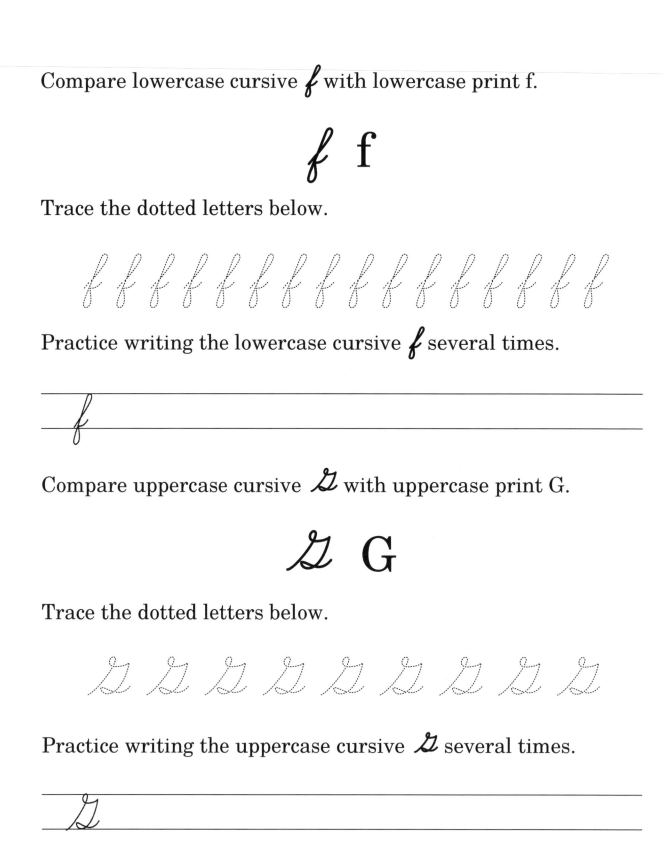

𝑓 f

Trace the dotted letters below.

Practice writing the lowercase cursive *f* several times.

Compare uppercase cursive *G* with uppercase print G.

G G

Trace the dotted letters below.

Practice writing the uppercase cursive *G* several times.

Compare uppercase cursive $\mathcal{I}$ with uppercase print I.

$\mathcal{I}$ I

Trace the dotted letters below.

Practice writing the uppercase cursive $\mathcal{I}$ several times.

Compare uppercase cursive $\mathcal{J}$ with uppercase print J.

$\mathcal{J}$ J

Trace the dotted letters below.

Practice writing the uppercase cursive $\mathcal{J}$ several times.

Compare lowercase cursive *j* with lowercase print j.

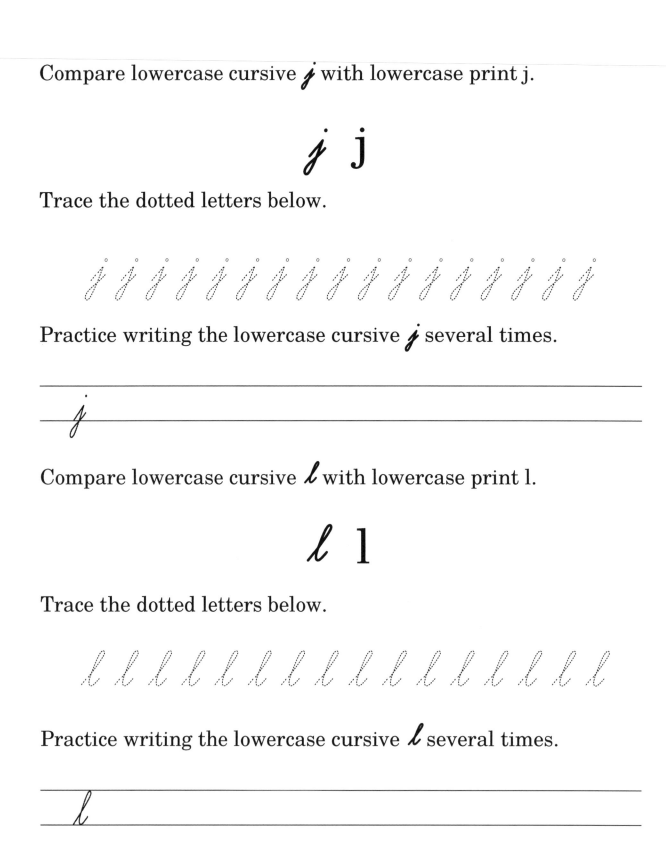

j j

Trace the dotted letters below.

Practice writing the lowercase cursive *j* several times.

Compare lowercase cursive *l* with lowercase print l.

l l

Trace the dotted letters below.

Practice writing the lowercase cursive *l* several times.

Compare lowercase cursive *m* with lowercase print m.

m m

Trace the dotted letters below.

m *m* *m* *m* *m* *m* *m* *m* *m*

Practice writing the lowercase cursive *m* several times.

m

Compare lowercase cursive *n* with lowercase print n.

n n

Trace the dotted letters below.

n *n* *n* *n* *n* *n* *n* *n* *n* *n*

Practice writing the lowercase cursive *n* several times.

n

Compare uppercase cursive $\mathcal{Q}$ with uppercase print Q.

$\mathcal{Q}$ Q

Trace the dotted letters below.

$\mathcal{Q}$ $\mathcal{Q}$ $\mathcal{Q}$ $\mathcal{Q}$ $\mathcal{Q}$ $\mathcal{Q}$ $\mathcal{Q}$ $\mathcal{Q}$ $\mathcal{Q}$ $\mathcal{Q}$ $\mathcal{Q}$ $\mathcal{Q}$

Practice writing the uppercase cursive $\mathcal{Q}$ several times.

Compare lowercase cursive n with lowercase print r.

n r

Trace the dotted letters below.

Practice writing the lowercase cursive n several times.

Compare uppercase cursive $\mathscr{S}$ with uppercase print S.

$\mathscr{S}$ S

Trace the dotted letters below.

Practice writing the uppercase cursive $\mathscr{S}$ several times.

Compare lowercase cursive s with lowercase print s.

s S

Trace the dotted letters below.

Practice writing the lowercase cursive s several times.

Compare lowercase cursive *u* with lowercase print v.

u V

Trace the dotted letters below.

u u u u u u u u u u u u u

Practice writing the lowercase cursive *u* several times.

u

Compare uppercase cursive *Y* with uppercase print Y.

Y Y

Trace the dotted letters below.

Y Y Y Y Y Y Y Y Y Y Y Y

Practice writing the uppercase cursive *Y* several times.

Compare uppercase cursive  with uppercase print Z.

Trace the dotted letters below.

Practice writing the uppercase cursive ℨ several times.

Compare lowercase cursive ℨ with lowercase print z.

ℨ   **Z**

Trace the dotted letters below.

Practice writing the lowercase cursive ℨ several times.

Another way that cursive letters can seem tricky is when two or more letters have a similar appearance.

For example, compare the uppercase cursive $\mathcal{L}$ to the uppercase cursive $\mathcal{S}$. When you see these letters side by side, it's clear that they are different. When students encounter one of these letters by itself and cursive handwriting is new to them, students sometimes forget which letter is which.

$$\mathcal{L} \quad \mathcal{S}$$

When two or more cursive letters have a similar appearance, it's important to remember which is which. The more time you spend studying the differences and practice writing the letters, the easier it will be to distinguish between similar letters.

If you read cursive writing that was written by somebody's hand, it can be even more difficult to distinguish between similar letters. A sloppy cursive $\mathcal{L}$ might look even more like a cursive $\mathcal{S}$, for example. The better your penmanship, the easier it will be for other people to read your handwriting.

Compare the cursive letters for uppercase D, G, and S.

$$\mathcal{D} \quad \mathcal{G} \quad \mathcal{S}$$

Trace the dotted letters below.

Practice writing each of these cursive letters multiple times.

Compare the cursive letters for lowercase f and uppercase J.

$$f \quad \mathcal{J}$$

Trace the dotted letters below.

Practice writing each of these cursive letters multiple times.

Compare the cursive letters for lowercase m and n.

m n

Trace the dotted letters below.

m n m n m n m n m n

Practice writing each of these cursive letters multiple times.

_____

_____

Remember that the lowercase cursive *m* has three humps, whereas the lowercase print m has two humps. Similarly, the lowercase cursive *n* has two humps, whereas the lowercase print n has one hump.

Also remember that the lowercase cursive *m* and *n* each have one more hump than the uppercase *M* and *N*. Examine the letters below closely.

M m N n

Compare the cursive letters for lowercase e and l and the cursive letter for uppercase I.

e l I

Trace the dotted letters below.

e l I e l I e l I e l I e l I

Practice writing each of these cursive letters multiple times.

_____

_____

Compare the cursive letters for lowercase u, v, and w.

u v w

Trace the dotted letters below.

u v w u v w u v w u v w

Practice writing each of these cursive letters multiple times.

_____

_____

Compare the cursive letters for uppercase I and J.

I J

Trace the dotted letters below.

I J I J I J I J I J I J I J I J

Practice writing each of these cursive letters multiple times.

_____

_____

Compare the cursive letters for uppercase Q, Y, and Z.

Q Y Z

Trace the dotted letters below.

Q Y Z Q Y Z Q Y Z Q Y Z

Practice writing each of these cursive letters multiple times.

_____

_____

Compare the cursive letters for lowercase r and s.

n s

Trace the dotted letters below.

n s n s n s n s n s n s n s

Practice writing each of these cursive letters multiple times.

_____

_____

Compare the cursive letters for lowercase g, p, and q.

g p q

Trace the dotted letters below.

g p q g p q g p q g p q g p q

Practice writing each of these cursive letters multiple times.

_____

_____

Compare the cursive letters for uppercase i and j.

i j

Trace the dotted letters below.

i j i j i j i j i j i j i j

Practice writing each of these cursive letters multiple times.

Compare the cursive letters for lowercase a and o.

a o

Trace the dotted letters below.

a o a o a o a o a o a o a o

Practice writing each of these cursive letters multiple times.

There is something a little tricky to many students about the uppercase cursive $\mathcal{D}$. It's not so much the way the letter looks that is the problem because the uppercase cursive $\mathcal{D}$ is similar in appearance to the uppercase print D.

$$\mathcal{D} \quad \mathrm{D}$$

What is tricky about the uppercase cursive $\mathcal{D}$ for some students is the way that the letter is written. In cursive, we first draw down the left side, and then finish by going up the right side. In print, it's common to draw down both the left and right sides. Compare the illustrations below.

We write the uppercase cursive $\mathcal{D}$ differently in cursive so that we can write the letter with a single smooth motion rather than two separate strokes.

Unfortunately, not everyone writes all of the letters of the uppercase and lowercase alphabet the exact same way. This varies partly with when and where people learned how to write in cursive, but even when two people learned cursive handwriting the same way, they still develop differences in their handwriting styles.

For example, consider the two common variations of the uppercase cursive *Q* shown below. Each cursive *Q* below corresponds to the uppercase print Q.

Q Q

We will point out a couple of the noteworthy differences. (It wouldn't be feasible to try to list every possible case.)

This adds to the challenge of reading cursive handwriting. When you write in cursive, the most important thing is to make your letters appear legible, so that other people can figure out which letter is which, even if they learned the cursive alphabet a little differently.

In the United States, it's traditional for the uppercase cursive *A* to look like a taller version of the lowercase cursive *a.* Occasionally, this letter is drawn to appear like an uppercase print A.

$$A \quad a$$

There are two common ways to write an uppercase cursive *H.* A benefit to the way it is drawn below on the right is that the letter can be made in two separate motions rather than three.

$$H \quad H$$

Some people draw an uppercase cursive *Q* so that it looks more like the uppercase print Q. Other people start the motion closer to the top of the letter so that it looks more like the number 2. The letters on the left and right below show the two extreme variations.

$$Q \quad Q \quad 2$$

Certain lowercase letters look different when they appear connected together in a word compared to how they look when drawn alone. The following letters gain a little connector at the left when they follow another letter to which they connect.

$$a \; c \; d \; g \; o \; q$$

These little connectors help these letters form cursive words. You can see this in the word "goal" below.

$$g \; + \; o \; + \; a \; + \; l \; = \; goal$$

Note that the lowercase cursive g doesn't gain a connector in the word "goal" because it is the first letter of the word. Contrast this with the word "egg" below, where the lowercase cursive g does gain a connector.

$$e \; + \; g \; + \; g \; = \; egg$$

Lowercase letters besides a, c, d, g, o, and q don't gain connectors. For example, the lowercase cursive l in the word "goal" makes a natural connection.

Trace the dotted letters below.

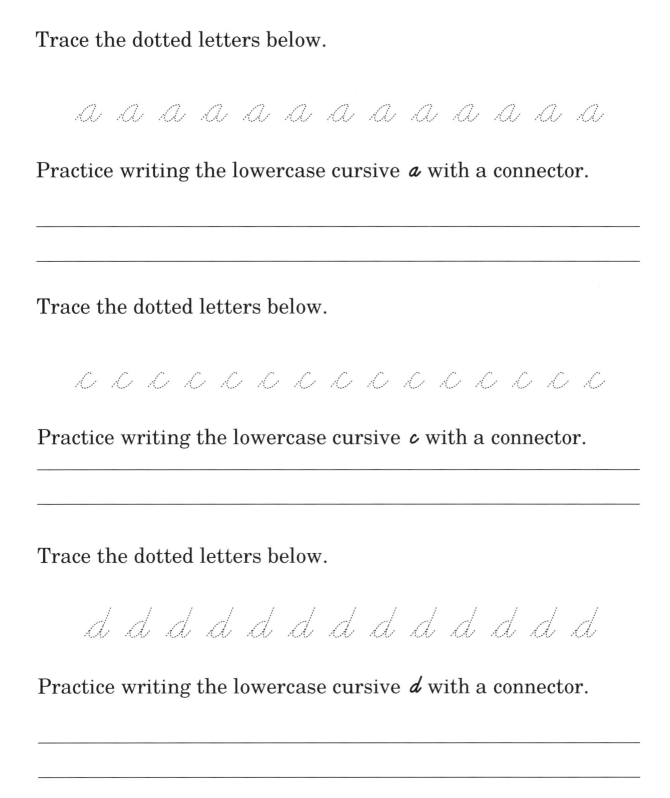

Practice writing the lowercase cursive *a* with a connector.

Trace the dotted letters below.

Practice writing the lowercase cursive *c* with a connector.

Trace the dotted letters below.

Practice writing the lowercase cursive *d* with a connector.

Trace the dotted letters below.

g g g g g g g g g g g g g g g

Practice writing the lowercase cursive *g* with a connector.

_____

_____

Trace the dotted letters below.

a a a a a a a a a a a a a a a

Practice writing the lowercase cursive *a* with a connector.

_____

_____

Trace the dotted letters below.

q q q q q q q q q q q q q q q

Practice writing the lowercase cursive *q* with a connector.

_____

_____

Some uppercase cursive letters connect with lowercase letters that follow them, while other uppercase cursive letters don't make a connection. Which uppercase cursive letters do or don't make a connection depend on the style of cursive handwriting being used. In this workbook, the following uppercase cursive letters don't connect to lowercase letters that follow them.

$$\mathcal{B} \quad \mathcal{D} \quad \mathcal{F} \quad \mathcal{I} \quad \mathcal{O} \quad \mathcal{P} \quad \mathcal{T} \quad \mathcal{V} \quad \mathcal{W}$$

For example, the uppercase cursive $\mathcal{W}$ doesn't connect to the lowercase cursive h in the word "Why."

$$\mathit{Why}$$

Other uppercase cursive letters naturally connect to lowercase letters that follow them in a capitalized word. For example, the uppercase cursive $\mathcal{C}$ naturally connects to the lowercase cursive a in the word "Connect."

$$\mathit{Connect}$$

Trace the dotted words below.

Art Blue Cat Dog

Copy the previous cursive words in the space below.

_____

_____

Trace the dotted words below.

Easy Fly Good Hard

Copy the previous cursive words in the space below.

_____

_____

Trace the dotted words below.

It Jewel Know Learn

Copy the previous cursive words in the space below.

_____

_____

Trace the dotted words below.

My New One Play Quiet

Copy the previous cursive words in the space below.

_____

_____

Trace the dotted words below.

Red Sweet Two Usual Van

Copy the previous cursive words in the space below.

_____

_____

Trace the dotted words below.

What Xylophone You Zoo

Copy the previous cursive words in the space below.

_____

_____

When a letter comes after a lowercase cursive *b*, it looks a little different than it normally does because it has to start higher. Look at the tail where the lowercase cursive *b* ends.

b f t

See how it finishes a little higher than where other lowercase cursive letters finish. Look closely at the right tails of the lowercase letters *b*, *f*, and *t* shown above.

b + *r* + *oom* = *broom*

f + *r* + *ee* = *free*

In the example above, you can see how the lowercase cursive *b* connects differently to the lowercase cursive *r* in the word "broom" compared to how the lowercase cursive *f* connects to the lowercase cursive *r* in the word "free." We will get some practice blending the lowercase cursive *b* with other letters in Chapter 4.

Letters that are rarely used in the English language can be hard to remember. For example, a capital Q is rarely used. Study or practice these letters in order to remember them better.

Trace the dotted uppercase and lowercase cursive *J* and *j*.

Copy the previous cursive words in the space below.

Trace the dotted uppercase and lowercase cursive *Q* and *q*.

Copy the previous cursive words in the space below.

Trace the dotted uppercase and lowercase cursive $\mathcal{V}$ and u.

$\mathcal{V}\ u\ \mathcal{V}\ u\ \mathcal{V}\ u\ \mathcal{V}\ u\ \mathcal{V}\ u\ \mathcal{V}\ u\ \mathcal{V}\ u$

Copy the previous cursive words in the space below.

Trace the dotted uppercase and lowercase cursive $\mathcal{X}$ and x.

$\mathcal{X}\ x\ \mathcal{X}\ x\ \mathcal{X}\ x\ \mathcal{X}\ x\ \mathcal{X}\ x\ \mathcal{X}\ x$

Copy the previous cursive words in the space below.

Trace the dotted uppercase and lowercase cursive $\mathcal{Z}$ and z.

$\mathcal{Z}\ z\ \mathcal{Z}\ z\ \mathcal{Z}\ z\ \mathcal{Z}\ z\ \mathcal{Z}\ z\ \mathcal{Z}\ z\ \mathcal{Z}\ z$

Copy the previous cursive words in the space below.

3

Memorize the Letters

Directions:

1. Write the answer to each exercise in the space provided.

2. These exercises are designed to help you remember the uppercase and lowercase cursive alphabet.

3. If you forget how to write a letter, review the diagram from Chapter 1 that shows how to write the letter.

4. Study the uppercase and lowercase cursive letters until you can both recognize each letter by sight and write each letter from memory. This is essential toward reading and writing cursive.

Study the uppercase cursive alphabet below. Try your best to memorize how each letter looks. Copy each letter onto the blank line below.

a B C D E F G

H I J K L M

n O P Q R S T

U V W X Y Z

Study the lowercase cursive alphabet below. Try your best to memorize how each letter looks. Copy each letter onto the blank line below.

a   b   c   d   e   f   g

h   i   j   k   l   m

n   o   p   q   r   s   t

u   v   w   x   y   z

The chart below shows which uppercase cursive and print letters go together. Refer to this chart to check your answers to the exercises that follow.

A = $\mathcal{A}$ B = $\mathcal{B}$ C = $\mathcal{C}$ D = $\mathcal{D}$

E = $\mathcal{E}$ F = $\mathcal{F}$ G = $\mathcal{G}$ H = $\mathcal{H}$

I = $\mathcal{I}$ J = $\mathcal{J}$ K = $\mathcal{K}$ L = $\mathcal{L}$

M = $\mathcal{M}$ N = $\mathcal{N}$ O = $\mathcal{O}$ P = $\mathcal{P}$

Q = $\mathcal{Q}$ R = $\mathcal{R}$ S = $\mathcal{S}$ T = $\mathcal{T}$

U = $\mathcal{U}$ V = $\mathcal{V}$ W = $\mathcal{W}$

X = $\mathcal{X}$ Y = $\mathcal{Y}$ Z = $\mathcal{Z}$

The chart below shows which lowercase cursive and print letters go together. Refer to this chart to check your answers to the exercises that follow.

a = *a*   b = *b*   c = *c*   d = *d*

e = *e*   f = *f*   g = *g*   h = *h*

i = *i*   j = *j*   k = *k*   l = *l*

m = *m*   n = *n*   o = *o*   p = *p*

q = *q*   r = *r*   s = *s*   t = *t*

u = *u*   v = *v*   w = *w*

x = *x*   y = *y*   z = *z*

The following exercises give you a cursive letter. Write the print letter that matches the given cursive letter.

Which print letter matches uppercase cursive $\mathcal{H}$?

———

———

Which print letter matches uppercase cursive $\mathcal{L}$?

———

———

Which print letter matches uppercase cursive $\mathcal{J}$?

———

———

Which print letter matches uppercase cursive $\mathcal{F}$?

———

———

Which print letter matches uppercase cursive $\mathcal{L}$?

———

———

Check your answers by referring to the chart on pages 94-95.

The following exercises give you a cursive letter. Write the print letter that matches the given cursive letter.

Which print letter matches uppercase cursive *A*?

——

——

Which print letter matches uppercase cursive *D*?

——

——

Which print letter matches uppercase cursive *F*?

——

——

Which print letter matches uppercase cursive *Q*?

——

——

Which print letter matches uppercase cursive *L*?

——

——

Check your answers by referring to the chart on pages 94-95.

The following exercises give you a cursive letter. Write the print letter that matches the given cursive letter.

Which print letter matches lowercase cursive *n*?

_____

_____

Which print letter matches lowercase cursive *b*?

_____

_____

Which print letter matches lowercase cursive *f*?

_____

_____

Which print letter matches lowercase cursive *s*?

_____

_____

Which print letter matches lowercase cursive *g*?

_____

_____

Check your answers by referring to the chart on page 94-95.

The following exercises give you a cursive letter. Write the print letter that matches the given cursive letter.

Which print letter matches lowercase cursive *m*?

_____

_____

Which print letter matches lowercase cursive *n*?

_____

_____

Which print letter matches lowercase cursive *e*?

_____

_____

Which print letter matches lowercase cursive *l*?

_____

_____

Which print letter matches lowercase cursive *u*?

_____

_____

Check your answers by referring to the chart on page 94-95.

The following exercises give you a printed letter. Write the cursive letter that matches the given printed letter.

Which cursive letter matches uppercase print D?

———

———

Which cursive letter matches uppercase print R?

———

———

Which cursive letter matches uppercase print G?

———

———

Which cursive letter matches uppercase print Y?

———

———

Which cursive letter matches uppercase print N?

———

———

Check your answers by referring to the chart on pages 94-95.

The following exercises give you a printed letter. Write the cursive letter that matches the given printed letter.

Which cursive letter matches uppercase print E?

_____

_____

Which cursive letter matches uppercase print I?

_____

_____

Which cursive letter matches uppercase print Z?

_____

_____

Which cursive letter matches uppercase print Q?

_____

_____

Which cursive letter matches uppercase print J?

_____

_____

Check your answers by referring to the chart on pages 94-95.

The following exercises give you a printed letter. Write the cursive letter that matches the given printed letter.

Which cursive letter matches lowercase print e?

_____

_____

Which cursive letter matches lowercase print i?

_____

_____

Which cursive letter matches lowercase print l?

_____

_____

Which cursive letter matches lowercase print m?

_____

_____

Which cursive letter matches lowercase print n?

_____

_____

Check your answers by referring to the chart on pages 94-95.

The following exercises give you a printed letter. Write the cursive letter that matches the given printed letter.

Which cursive letter matches lowercase print b?

_____

_____

Which cursive letter matches lowercase print j?

_____

_____

Which cursive letter matches lowercase print r?

_____

_____

Which cursive letter matches lowercase print s?

_____

_____

Which cursive letter matches lowercase print z?

_____

_____

Check your answers by referring to the chart on pages 94-95.

Now try writing the uppercase cursive alphabet from memory. Below each print letter, write the corresponding cursive letter.

A B C D E F G

_____

_____

H I J K L M

_____

_____

N O P Q R S T

_____

_____

U V W X Y Z

_____

_____

Check your answers by comparing with page 92.

Now try writing the lowercase cursive alphabet from memory. Below each print letter, write the corresponding cursive letter.

a b c d e f g

_____

_____

h i j k l m

_____

_____

n o p q r s t

_____

_____

u v w x y z

_____

_____

Check your answers by comparing with page 93.

Which letters seemed more challenging to you? Practice writing these letters several times in the space provided. Writing can help with memory. Study these letters.

_____

_____

_____

_____

_____

_____

_____

_____

_____

_____

_____

_____

_____

4

Forming Cursive Words

Directions:

1. Study how the cursive letters connect together.

2. First practice by tracing over the dotted letters or words.

3. Next copy the letters or words onto the blank line below.

4. It may help to review the issues discussed in Chapter 2.

5. Focus on writing smoothly without lifting your pencil (except for certain uppercase letters). If your letters come out a little different, it may be okay. The most important thing is that other people can read your writing.

Cursive letters connect together when they form words. You can see this in the word "chain" below.

$$c + h + a + i + n = chain$$

As we noted in Chapter 2, the following lowercase letters gain a little connector at the left when they follow another letter, while the other lowercase letters make a natural connection. See how the lowercase cursive *a* gains a connector in the word "chain," while the lowercase cursive *c* doesn't gain a connector because it begins the word.

$$a \ c \ d \ g \ o \ q$$

Note how all of the letters in the word "time" below connect naturally, whereas the "a" in the word "chain" above gains a special connector.

$$t + i + m + e = time$$

Also recall from Chapter 2 that the following uppercase letters don't make a connection, while the other uppercase letters make a natural connection.

$$\mathcal{B} \quad \mathcal{D} \quad \mathcal{F} \quad \mathcal{I} \quad \mathcal{O} \quad \mathcal{P} \quad \mathcal{T} \quad \mathcal{V} \quad \mathcal{W}$$

Following are a few examples of capitalized cursive words.

$$C + a + r + o + l = Carol$$

$$\mathcal{F} + r + a + n + c + e = France$$

$$\mathcal{G} + a + r + y = Gary$$

$$\mathcal{I} + o + w + a = Iowa$$

$$\mathcal{T} + o + m = Tom$$

Note how "France," "Iowa," and "Tom" have little gaps after the first letter, unlike "Carol" and "Gary."

First trace the letters and then copy them onto the blank lines.

The exercises below involve the pair of letters "ac."

Ac ac ac Ac ac ac Ac ac ac

_____

_____

Act fact race Acorn pack ace

_____

_____

The exercises below involve the pair of letters "an."

An an an An an an An an an

_____

_____

Any can than And sand clean

_____

_____

First trace the letters and then copy them onto the blank lines.

The exercises below involve the pair of letters "ar."

Ar ar ar Ar ar ar Ar ar ar

_____

_____

Art heart care Army star warm

_____

_____

The exercises below involve the pair of letters "at."

At at at At at at At at at

_____

_____

Ate hat math Atlas cat eat

_____

_____

We discussed the lowercase cursive *b* briefly in Chapter 2. When a letter comes after a lowercase cursive *b*, the letter after the *b* looks a little different because it has to start higher. In each of the examples below, look closely at how the second letter of the word looks. You should see that it starts a little higher when the first letter is a lowercase cursive *b*.

bag   tag

bed   red

bike   like

blue   glue

book   cook

brain   train

First trace the letters and then copy them onto the blank lines.

The exercises below involve the pair of letters "bl."

Bl bl bl Bl bl bl Bl bl bl

_____

_____

Blue table double Black cable

_____

_____

The exercises below involve the pair of letters "br."

Br br br Br br br Br br br

_____

_____

Brown bring Bright break

_____

_____

First trace the letters and then copy them onto the blank lines.

The exercises below involve the pair of letters "ch."

Ch ch ch Ch ch ch Ch ch ch

_____

_____

Cheese reach Church lunch much

_____

_____

The exercises below involve the pair of letters "cl."

Cl cl cl Cl cl cl Cl cl cl Cl cl cl

_____

_____

Clue bicycle Clean clever clown

_____

_____

First trace the letters and then copy them onto the blank lines.

The exercises below involve the pair of letters "de."

De de de De de de De de de

The exercises below involve the pair of letters "dr."

Dr dr dr Dr dr dr Dr dr dr

Dry dragon Dream drum drink

Some people smooth out the lowercase cursive *e* such that it appears more like a shorter version of the cursive *l*. Compare the two pictures below.

l   *l*

This may make it more natural or efficient to write lowercase cursive *e*, but if you choose to write it this way, you need to be careful that your letter is legible. If you accidentally make it a little too tall, for example, it could be confused with a lowercase cursive *l*.

Use the blank lines below to practice writing the lowercase cursive *e* several times. See which style you feel comfortable with. Examine your writing to see if it looks legible to you. Better yet, seek the opinion of someone who is familiar with cursive handwriting.

_____

___*l*_____

_____

___*l*_____

First trace the letters and then copy them onto the blank lines.

The exercises below involve the pair of letters "ed."

Ed ed ed Ed ed ed Ed ed ed

Edge ruled fled Edit seed cried

The exercises below involve the pair of letters "en."

En en en En en en En en en

Enjoy ten sent England green

First trace the letters and then copy them onto the blank lines.

The exercises below involve the pair of letters "fa."

Fa fa fa Fa fa fa Fa fa fa

_____

_____

Father fast fan Far fame farm

_____

_____

The exercises below involve the pair of letters "fl."

Fl fl fl Fl fl fl Fl fl fl

_____

_____

Flower flame Floor waffle

_____

_____

First trace the letters and then copy them onto the blank lines.

The exercises below involve the pair of letters "go."

Go go go Go go go Go go go

_____

_____

Good golf goose Gone goat

_____

_____

The exercises below involve the pair of letters "gr."

Gr gr gr Gr gr gr Gr gr gr

_____

_____

Green angry Gray hungry

_____

_____

First trace the letters and then copy them onto the blank lines.

The exercises below involve the pair of letters "ha."

Ha ha ha Ha ha ha Ha ha ha

Half chair shark Happen than

The exercises below involve the pair of letters "hi."

Hi hi hi Hi hi hi Hi hi hi

High this chin Hip shirt thing

The uppercase cursive *I* doesn't really connect with a lowercase letter that follows it in the same word. When you first see a capitalized cursive word beginning with the letter *I*, it might seem like it "should" connect because the bottom right edge of the letter *I* is close to the bottom left edge of the lowercase letter that follows it. Note the small gap between the letters *I* and *s* in the word "Island" below.

Island

There is a good reason for the small gap: It's because we actually draw the uppercase cursive *I* right to left instead of from left to right. See the arrows below.

There really is no harm in making the uppercase cursive *I* connect with the following letter. In fact, the writing might look prettier if it does connect. It isn't a natural connection though, so it would take a little extra time and effort to do this. Remember, cursive handwriting is designed to save time.

First trace the letters and then copy them onto the blank lines.

The exercises below involve the pair of letters "in."

In in in In in in In in in

_____

_____

Instant singing Information

_____

_____

The exercises below involve the pair of letters "jo."

Jo jo jo Jo jo jo Jo jo jo

_____

_____

Joke enjoy Job banjo jogger

_____

_____

First trace the letters and then copy them onto the blank lines.

The exercises below involve the pair of letters "kn."

Kn kn kn Kn kn kn

_____

_____

Know knickknack Knew

_____

_____

The exercises below involve the pair of letters "lu."

Lu lu lu Lu lu lu Lu lu lu

_____

_____

Luck club plum Lunch blue

_____

_____

First trace the letters and then copy them onto the blank lines.

The exercises below involve the pair of letters "me."

Me me me Me me me

The exercises below involve the pair of letters "nd."

nd nd nd nd nd nd nd nd

and find candy bend sand

First trace the letters and then copy them onto the blank lines.

The exercises below involve the pair of letters "oc."

Oc oc oc Oc oc oc Oc oc oc

_____

_____

Ocean rock soccer Octagon

_____

_____

The exercises below involve the pair of letters "ph."

Ph ph ph Ph ph ph Ph ph ph

_____

_____

Phone graph Phonics trophy

_____

_____

First trace the letters and then copy them onto the blank lines.

The exercises below involve the pair of letters "qu."

Qu qu qu Qu qu qu Qu qu qu

Queen quite quiet Quest quote

The exercises below involve the pair of letters "rt."

rt rt rt rt rt rt rt rt rt rt rt

start fort party court art worth

First trace the letters and then copy them onto the blank lines.

The exercises below involve the pair of letters "sh."

Sh sh sh Sh sh sh Sh sh sh

_____

_____

Share dish wash Shape flash

_____

_____

The exercises below involve the pair of letters "st."

St st st St st st St st st

_____

_____

Stripe best fast Stink trust

_____

_____

First trace the letters and then copy them onto the blank lines.

The exercises below involve the pair of letters "te."

Te te te Te te te Te te te

_____

_____

Teach taste better Test steer

_____

_____

The exercises below involve the pair of letters "th."

Th th th Th th th Th th th

_____

_____

The fifth other Thursday three

_____

_____

First trace the letters and then copy them onto the blank lines.

The exercises below involve the pair of letters "un."

Un un un Un un un

_____

_____

Unique fun run Under sunshine

_____

_____

The exercises below involve the pair of letters "ve."

Ve ve ve Ve ve ve Ve ve ve

_____

_____

Very have behave Vest give

_____

_____

Similar to the lowercase cursive *b*, which we discussed on page 112, when a letter comes after a lowercase cursive *w*, the letter after the *w* looks a little different because it has to start higher. In each of the examples below, look closely at how the second letter of the word looks. You should see that it starts a little higher when the first letter is a lowercase cursive *w*.

walk talk

week seek

what that

win pin

would could

wry try

First trace the letters and then copy them onto the blank lines.

The exercises below involve the pair of letters "wa."

Wa wa wa Wa wa wa

_____

_____

Water away swam Wait sway

_____

_____

The exercises below involve the pair of letters "wh."

Wh wh wh Wh wh wh

_____

_____

Whale what who Whole white

_____

_____

First trace the letters and then copy them onto the blank lines.

The exercises below involve the pair of letters "wn."

wn wn wn wn wn wn wn

_____

_____

town pawn grown lawn dawn

_____

_____

The exercises below involve the pair of letters "ws."

ws ws ws ws ws ws ws ws

_____

_____

claws glows paws sews grows

_____

_____

First trace the letters and then copy them onto the blank lines.

The exercises below involve the pair of letters "wr."

Wr wr wr Wr wr wr

Wrong wreck Wrestle write

The exercises below involve the pair of letters "xe."

xe xe xe xe xe xe xe xe xe xe xe

taxes fixed oxen boxer foxes

First trace the letters and then copy them onto the blank lines.

The exercises below involve the pair of letters "ye."

Ye ye ye Ye ye ye Ye ye ye

_____

_____

Yes eye yet Year eyeball yell

_____

_____

The exercises below involve the pair of letters "ze."

Ze ze ze Ze ze ze Ze ze ze

_____

_____

Zebra breeze Zest prize size

_____

_____

5

Copy Sentences

Directions:

1. This chapter isn't designed for tracing.

2. Copy each sentence onto the blank line below.

3. Focus on writing smoothly without lifting your pencil between words (except for certain uppercase letters). If your letters come out a little different, it may be okay. The most important thing is that other people can read your writing.

Apples crunch between teeth.

Butterflies dance in the wind.

Class begins when the bell rings.

Drink a cup of hot chocolate.

Enjoy an hour of relaxing music.

Feel cozy in a soft blanket.

Goosebumps form on cold skin.

Hear a rooster crow at sunrise.

Imagine a great big smile.

Jingling keys please babies.

Keep warm by a fireplace.

Listen to the raindrops fall.

Music boxes play soft tunes.

Neon lights shine bright at night.

Ocean waves splash on the shore.

Photographs store fond memories.

Quietly tiptoe through the house.

Read a story to a child.

Smell roses when they bloom.

Taste freshly baked brownies.

Umbrellas provide a little shelter.

Vegetables come in different colors.

Worms wriggle across the ground.

Yo-yos wind up and down.

Zoo animals make many sounds.

The apes ate apples and bananas.

We blew bubbles by the barn.

He ate chocolate chip ice-cream.

I fed bread to ducks at a pond.

She likes to eat cheddar cheese.

The first leaf fell from the tree.

Our dog is begging to go out.

The highway has many potholes.

It is time to listen to music.

He just juggled six jars of jelly.

The kids like to play kickball.

I will call at eleven o'clock.

Remember sweet memories.

Enjoy the sunset in the evening.

Food looks good in your cookbook.

Puppies played peek-a-boo.

Students take quizzes quietly.

Red carpet covers our floor.

Sugar cookies taste so sweet.

Two kittens tugged on the string.

May I get under your umbrella?

We were invited to a wedding.

The waiter wore a tuxedo.

Schedule your eye exam.

Your prize is a slice of pizza.

If you look closely enough, you can find art in anything.

A sculptor can start with a block of stone and transform it into a three-dimensional creation.

Poets see art in the many ways
that they weave words together.

Architects find art in the design
of buildings and other physical
structures.

Musicians create art that you can appreciate with your ears.

_____

_____

_____

_____

Dancers feel the art of music in their muscles, while also creating their own visual displays of art.

_____

_____

_____

_____

Many writers strive to perfect the art of telling a great story.

Physicists find beauty while attempting to unravel the many mysteries of the universe.

Engineers see art in technology and its applications.

From ocean waves to beehives to rock formations to butterflies, nature is filled with art forms.

Archaeologists dig up ancient
works of art.

Mathematicians find beauty in
numerical patterns and the
relationships among numbers.

You can experience art through religion and spirituality.

There is even beauty to behold through the lenses of telescopes or microscopes.

6

Read and Write Cursive

Directions:

1. The exercises in the first half of this chapter give you a cursive word or sentence and ask you to write it in print. This will help you learn how to read cursive handwriting.

2. The exercises in the second half of this chapter give you a printed word or sentence and ask you to write it in cursive. This will help you learn how to write with cursive handwriting.

3. If you need help, consult the chart on pages 154-155.

The chart below shows which uppercase cursive and print letters go together. Refer to this chart if you need help remembering the uppercase letters.

A = $\mathcal{A}$ B = $\mathcal{B}$ C = $\mathcal{C}$ D = $\mathcal{D}$

E = $\mathcal{E}$ F = $\mathcal{F}$ G = $\mathcal{G}$ H = $\mathcal{H}$

I = $\mathcal{I}$ J = $\mathcal{J}$ K = $\mathcal{K}$ L = $\mathcal{L}$

M = $\mathcal{M}$ N = $\mathcal{N}$ O = $\mathcal{O}$ P = $\mathcal{P}$

Q = $\mathcal{Q}$ R = $\mathcal{R}$ S = $\mathcal{S}$ T = $\mathcal{T}$

U = $\mathcal{U}$ V = $\mathcal{V}$ W = $\mathcal{W}$

X = $\mathcal{X}$ Y = $\mathcal{Y}$ Z = $\mathcal{Z}$

The chart below shows which lowercase cursive and print letters go together. Refer to this chart if you need help remembering the lowercase letters.

a = *a*   b = *b*   c = *c*   d = *d*

e = *e*   f = *f*   g = *g*   h = *h*

i = *i*   j = *j*   k = *k*   l = *l*

m = *m*   n = *n*   o = *o*   p = *p*

q = *q*   r = *r*   s = *s*   t = *t*

u = *u*   v = *v*   w = *w*

x = *x*   y = *y*   z = *z*

The following exercises give you a cursive word. Rewrite the word in print. The first exercise is done as an example.

Write the cursive word *flower* in print.

<u>flower</u>

Write the cursive word *three* in print.

Write the cursive word *whale* in print.

Write the cursive word *zebra* in print.

Write the cursive word *share* in print.

Check your answers by referring to page 164.

The following exercises give you a cursive word. Rewrite the word in print.

Write the cursive word *bounce* in print.

_____

_____

Write the cursive word *name* in print.

_____

_____

Write the cursive word *sun* in print.

_____

_____

Write the cursive word *quiet* in print.

_____

_____

Write the cursive word *grin* in print.

_____

_____

Check your answers by referring to page 164.

The following exercises give you a capitalized cursive name. Rewrite the name in print.

Write the cursive name *Mary* in print.

_____

_____

Write the cursive name *Paul* in print.

_____

_____

Write the cursive name *Rachel* in print.

_____

_____

Write the cursive name *Bobby* in print.

_____

_____

Write the cursive name *Nicole* in print.

_____

_____

Check your answers by referring to page 164.

The following exercises give you a capitalized cursive name. Rewrite the name in print.

Write the cursive name *John* in print.

_____

_____

Write the cursive name *Sarah* in print.

_____

_____

Write the cursive name *Eugene* in print.

_____

_____

Write the cursive name *Quince* in print.

_____

_____

Write the cursive name *Ingrid* in print.

_____

_____

Check your answers by referring to page 164.

The following exercises give you a printed word. Rewrite the word in cursive. The first exercise is done as an example.

Write the print word shine in cursive.

shine

Write the print word forest in cursive.

Write the print word beauty in cursive.

Write the print word rainbow in cursive.

Write the print word team in cursive.

Check your answers by referring to page 164.

The following exercises give you a printed word. Rewrite the word in cursive.

Write the print word house in cursive.

_____

_____

Write the print word video in cursive.

_____

_____

Write the print word unique in cursive.

_____

_____

Write the print word tower in cursive.

_____

_____

Write the print word prize in cursive.

_____

_____

Check your answers by referring to page 164.

The following exercises give you a capitalized printed name. Rewrite the name in cursive.

Write the print name Becky in cursive.

_____

_____

Write the print name Michael in cursive.

_____

_____

Write the print name Elizabeth in cursive.

_____

_____

Write the print name James in cursive.

_____

_____

Write the print name Irene in cursive.

_____

_____

Check your answers by referring to page 164.

The following exercises give you a capitalized printed name. Rewrite the name in cursive.

Write the print name Queen in cursive.

_____

_____

Write the print name Yvonne in cursive.

_____

_____

Write the print name Harry in cursive.

_____

_____

Write the print name Samantha in cursive.

_____

_____

Write the print name Zane in cursive.

_____

_____

Check your answers by referring to page 164.

Below are the answers to the exercises on pages 156-163.

Page 156:

  flower, three, whale, zebra, share

Page 157:

  bounce, name, sun, quiet, grin

Page 158:

  Mary, Paul, Rachel, Bobby, Nicole

Page 159:

  John, Sarah, Eugene, Quince, Ingrid

Page 160:

  shine, forest, beauty, rainbow, team

Page 161:

  house, video, unique, tower, prize

Page 162:

  Becky, Michael, Elizabeth, James, Irene

Page 163:

  Queen, Yvonne, Harry, Samantha, Zane

The following exercises give you sentences in cursive handwriting. Rewrite each sentence in print. The first exercise is done as an example.

Feel the pulse of your heartbeat.

Feel the pulse of your heartbeat.

Stretch your lower body muscles.

Dance to the rhythm of music.

Wave your arms in the air.

Check your answers by referring to page 171.

Lions chased zebras and gazelles.

Giraffes ate leaves off tall trees.

Cheetahs sprinted across the field.

A stampede of elephants went by.

The crocodiles waited in the river.

Check your answers by referring to page 171.

Kittens purred as we petted them.

Puppies ran fast chasing balls.

Parrots repeated our phrases.

We rode horses along the trail.

Our kids enjoyed the petting zoo.

Check your answers by referring to page 171.

Listen to ocean waves splash.

Watch the sun rise and set.

Feel the afternoon breeze.

Taste your favorite foods.

Smell the fruits and vegetables.

Check your answers by referring to page 172.

Visit with friends or relatives.

Learn how to do something new.

Quote great advice that you heard.

Go somewhere that is exciting.

Dream about a wonderful future.

Check your answers by referring to page 172.

Read an article in a newspaper.

_____

_____

Have an audio book read to you.

_____

_____

Attend a play at a local theatre.

_____

_____

Take part in a discussion group.

_____

_____

Visit a museum in a big city.

_____

_____

Check your answers by referring to page 172.

Below are the answers to the exercises on pages 165-167.

Page 165:

Feel the pulse of your heartbeat.

Stretch your lower body muscles.

Dance to the rhythm of music.

Wave your arms in the air.

Page 166:

Lions chased zebras and gazelles.

Giraffes ate leaves off tall trees.

Cheetahs sprinted across the field.

A stampede of elephants went by.

The crocodiles waited in the river.

Page 167:

Kittens purred as we petted them.

Puppies ran fast chasing balls.

Parrots repeated our phrases.

We rode horses along the trail.

Our kids enjoyed the petting zoo.

Below are the answers to the exercises on pages 168-170.

Page 168:

> Listen to ocean waves splash.
>
> Watch the sun rise and set.
>
> Feel the afternoon breeze.
>
> Taste your favorite foods.
>
> Smell the fruits and vegetables.

Page 169:

> Visit with friends or relatives.
>
> Learn how to do something new.
>
> Quote great advice that you heard.
>
> Go somewhere that is exciting.
>
> Dream about a wonderful future.

Page 170:

> Read an article in a newspaper.
>
> Have an audio book read to you.
>
> Attend a play at a local theatre.
>
> Take part in a discussion group.
>
> Visit a museum in a big city.

The following exercises give you printed sentences. Rewrite each sentence in cursive handwriting. The first exercise is done as an example.

Swim a few laps in the pool.

Swim a few laps in the pool.

Go jogging around the block.

Perform some daily exercises.

Keep active with a regular sport.

Check your answers by referring to page 179.

Solve a crossword puzzle.

_____

_____

Play cards with your friends.

_____

_____

Circle answers in a word search.

_____

_____

Relax with a coloring book.

_____

_____

Figure out a sudoku puzzle.

_____

_____

Check your answers by referring to page 179.

Enjoy dinner at a restaurant.

Watch a movie at a theatre.

Shop for some new clothes.

Take a vacation for a week.

Go camping in the wilderness.

Check your answers by referring to page 179.

Laugh hysterically for a while.

Breathe out a sigh of relief.

Wink your left eye for a moment.

Plaster a smile on your face.

Whistle a tune while you walk.

Check your answers by referring to page 180.

Clap your hands in delight.

Quickly snap your fingers.

Wave goodbye when you leave.

Blow a kiss through the air.

Jump up high with pure joy.

Check your answers by referring to page 180.

Once upon a time, there were...

_____

_____

It was a dark and stormy night...

_____

_____

Wake up and smell the coffee...

_____

_____

Arrived just in the nick of time...

_____

_____

And they lived happily ever after...

_____

_____

Check your answers by referring to page 180.

Below are the answers to the exercises on pages 173-175.

Page 173:

Swim a few laps in the pool.

Go jogging around the block.

Perform some daily exercises.

Keep active with a regular sport.

Page 174:

Solve a crossword puzzle.

Play cards with your friends.

Circle answers in a word search.

Relax with a coloring book.

Figure out a sudoku puzzle.

Page 175:

Enjoy dinner at a restaurant.

Watch a movie at a theatre.

Shop for some new clothes.

Take a vacation for a week.

Go camping in the wilderness.

Below are the answers to the exercises on pages 176-178.

Page 176:

> *Laugh hysterically for a while.*
>
> *Breathe out a sigh of relief.*
>
> *Wink your left eye for a moment.*
>
> *Plaster a smile on your face.*
>
> *Whistle a tune while you walk.*

Page 177:

> *Clap your hands in delight.*
>
> *Quickly snap your fingers.*
>
> *Wave goodbye when you leave.*
>
> *Blow a kiss through the air.*
>
> *Jump up high with pure joy.*

Page 178:

> *Once upon a time, there were...*
>
> *It was a dark and stormy night...*
>
> *Wake up and smell the coffee...*
>
> *Arrived just in the nick of time...*
>
> *And they lived happily ever after...*

7

Handwriting Prompts

Directions:

1. These exercises don't give you words to copy. Instead, they provide writing prompts.

2. Write about each writing prompt in the space provided.

3. Write with cursive handwriting.

4. If you forget how to write a letter, consult the chart on pages 182-183.

The chart below shows which uppercase cursive and print letters go together. Refer to this chart if you forget how to write one of the uppercase letters.

A = $\mathcal{A}$ B = $\mathcal{B}$ C = $\mathcal{C}$ D = $\mathcal{D}$

E = $\mathcal{E}$ F = $\mathcal{F}$ G = $\mathcal{G}$ H = $\mathcal{H}$

I = $\mathcal{I}$ J = $\mathcal{J}$ K = $\mathcal{K}$ L = $\mathcal{L}$

M = $\mathcal{M}$ N = $\mathcal{N}$ O = $\mathcal{O}$ P = $\mathcal{P}$

Q = $\mathcal{Q}$ R = $\mathcal{R}$ S = $\mathcal{S}$ T = $\mathcal{T}$

U = $\mathcal{U}$ V = $\mathcal{V}$ W = $\mathcal{W}$

X = $\mathcal{X}$ Y = $\mathcal{Y}$ Z = $\mathcal{Z}$

The chart below shows which lowercase cursive and print letters go together. Refer to this chart if you forget how to write one of the lowercase letters.

a = *a*   b = *b*   c = *c*   d = *d*

e = *e*   f = *f*   g = *g*   h = *h*

i = *i*   j = *j*   k = *k*   l = *l*

m = *m*   n = *n*   o = *o*   p = *p*

q = *q*   r = *r*   s = *s*   t = *t*

u = *u*   v = *v*   w = *w*

x = *x*   y = *y*   z = *z*

Write about a hobby that you enjoy.

_____

_____

_____

_____

_____

_____

_____

Write about a sport that you play or watch.

_____

_____

_____

_____

_____

_____

_____

Write about how you met one of your friends.

_____

_____

_____

_____

_____

_____

_____

Write about something that you did with a friend.

_____

_____

_____

_____

_____

_____

_____

Describe the weather outside today.

_____

_____

_____

_____

_____

_____

Describe how you are feeling today.

_____

_____

_____

_____

_____

_____

Describe a place that you enjoy visiting.

_____

_____

_____

_____

_____

_____

_____

Describe an event that happened in the past.

_____

_____

_____

_____

_____

_____

_____

Explain how to do something that you do well.

_____

_____

_____

_____

_____

_____

_____

Explain the answer to a problem that you solved.

_____

_____

_____

_____

_____

_____

_____

Explain your reasoning for an opinion that you hold.

_____

_____

_____

_____

_____

_____

_____

Explain how to make something.

_____

_____

_____

_____

_____

_____

_____

Describe an animal (real or imagined).

_____

_____

_____

_____

_____

_____

Describe a hero (real or imagined).

_____

_____

_____

_____

_____

_____

Describe an invention (real or imagined).

_____

_____

_____

_____

_____

_____

Describe a means of transportation (real or imagined).

_____

_____

_____

_____

_____

_____

Write about your favorite piece of clothing.

_____

_____

_____

_____

_____

_____

Write about your favorite food.

_____

_____

_____

_____

_____

_____

Write about a memory that makes you smile.

_____

_____

_____

_____

_____

_____

_____

Write about something that you enjoy doing.

_____

_____

_____

_____

_____

_____

_____

Keep Writing

The way to improve your handwriting skills and to maintain your fluency is to continue to practice writing regularly. Following are some suggestions to help you keep writing:

- Look for more cursive handwriting practice workbooks. Jenny Pearson will have more workbooks coming in the future. You can see her current publications at her Amazon author page:

  amazon.com/author/jennypearson

- Write daily in a journal or diary.

- Find a friend, relative, or pen pal that you can exchange handwritten letters with by mail.

- Search for inspirational quotes, or any writing you enjoy, and practice rewriting them in cursive.

- Write poems or stories.

- Anytime you need to write a note or a list, use cursive.

- See if you can write the uppercase and lowercase cursive alphabet from memory on a blank sheet of paper. When you finish, compare your work with page 60.

Coloring Books for Teens or Adults

Coloring books aren't just for kids. They are popular among teens and adults, too. Coloring provides a relaxing way to take your mind off of stress, and lets you use your creativity.

by Jenny Pearson

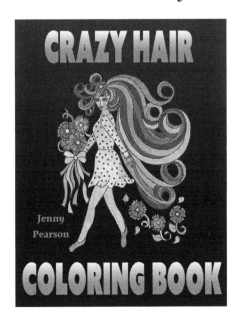
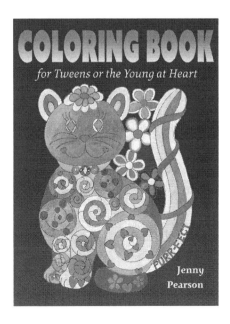

46727897R00110

Made in the USA
Middletown, DE
07 August 2017